KATHLEEN DENIZARD

ECHOES of NOW

Echoes of Now

Copyright © 2023 Kathleen Denizard

All rights reserved. Printed in the United States of America. No part of this book may be used or reproduced in any manner whatsoever without written permission except in the case of reprints in the context of reviews.

Wrinkled Sea Press
P.O. Box 234
S. Orleans, Massachusetts 02662

ISBN 978-1-7377477-3-4

Text and cover design by Charita Patamikakorn

Thanks to Paul Cordeiro for editorial guidance

Wrinkled Sea Press thanks Imspired Press for permission to publish
Walk With Me, Summer is Almost Over, Colors of Autumn, Bountiful,
Real Man in a Pink House, Yard Sale-ing, Bazaar Invitation,
Don't Call Me Late Anymore, Bed and Breakfast, Six Months Later,
Upon Our Visitor's Stopping, and Attic Man

PUBLISHER'S NOTE

Welcome to *Echoes of Now*, a collection of thirty-three poems and twelve narratives – indeed, a tapestry woven with words, where each thread is a verse.

The poetry and narrative within these covers are born from moments of quiet introspection; Kathleen Denizard's observations on the subtle play of light and shadow in our everyday lives, the complexity of human emotion, and the simple, often overlooked moments that stitch our days together.

Whether you find solace, inspiration, or a mirror to your own experiences, my hope is that they touch your heart in some way, reminding you of the beauty and depth of our trip through this sometimes-absurd universe.

Gerry Grenier
Wrinkled Sea Press
S. Orleans, MA

POETRY & NARRATIVE

Publisher's Note	iii	Up From the Beach	23
Sun Coming Up	1	Fishing	24
Morning	2	Brown Dog	25
Tiny Garden	3	Guest	26
Across the Miles	4	Keeping Cool	27
November	5	Walk With Me	28
Awaiting	6	Passage	30
Quiet	7	Solitary Gull	31
Sweet Moment Missed	8	Summer Is Almost Over	32
Photo	9	Colors of Autumn	33
Child Leaving	10	Bountiful	34
Celebration	11	For Heaven's Sake	35
Out of the Shower	12	Snow Shadow	36
Rude	13	Reaching the Channel	38
Winter Woe	14	Terminal	39
Ghost	15	Real Man in a Pink House?	40
Respite	16	Bazaar Invitation	41
Cookout	17	Yard Sale-ing	42
Workshop	18	Don't Call Me Late Anymore	44
Miss Priss	19	Bed and Breakfast	46
Open Mic	20	Six Months Later	48
Ask	21	Upon Our Visitor's Stopping	50
Fan Spirit	22	Attic Man	53

SUN COMING UP

Sleep comes hard
After the toil of day
After evening cocktails
And sweet good-nights
Not a night that settles in dreams of quiet
A surge of thoughts
Like an open spout, recalls the day
Of to-do-lists left undone
Reminding me of friends to see,
Business not realized
I toss about, ignoring another's hand in mine
Unable to feel any calm
Slippery with sweat. And no relief
The burn of wishes undone will not cool
Through an open window
The sun is rising with no let-up
Tomorrow is happening
Now

MORNING

Rain drizzling, fog rolling
Roses are drinking the dew
I feel the sun breaking through
Tugging the door open
Excited to pluck a blossom

TINY GARDEN

Looking out I caught my brother snipping tulips
    from his tiny garden
Hedged among so many pink and other little flowers
On his side of the window, he sees me watching
Knowing he would offer me a bag of petite peas
Tenderly grown on the sill

ACROSS THE MILES

You sent me a postcard
Of snowfall made for sledding
Of a snowman tall as the doorhead
I should be visiting you
But I will wait until the ponds thaw
And the forsythia bloom

NOVEMBER

When days grow short
I am lonely knowing
Nothing bright will grow
I feel the unforgiving wind
As cold as I am now

AWAITING

Up the street I hear a car rattle over cobblestones
I hope it's the postman coming to deliver
    the birthday card my mother sent
The one gifting relief for my electric bill tucked inside
An abrupt stomp on the brakes stops
    a familiar red, white and blue vehicle
At my mailbox
Quick hands drop whatever can be stuffed
    into the small portal
With an anxious grip pulling down the metal handle
I let the contents spill into my lap
Every envelope, each piece of advertisement was scanned
Until I was sure the card had not arrived
The wind is blowing into my midi skirt
Into my eyes now burning with disappointment
So, I turn from the wind knowing the postman
    will deliver again
Rattling his car over the cobblestone road tomorrow
And I will be waiting

QUIET

When I stamp the snow off my boots
I think of a snowy country road
Preferring the company of friends
Before the dogs come barking
Before snowblowers rev
I try not to listen
To the rapping of a woodpecker on a neighbor's house

SWEET MOMENT MISSED

On Christmas eve
Kids asleep, wrapping presents together
When I lean over to kiss you
A hand comes up out of your robe pocket to stop me
Pulling out chapstick to swipe dry lips

PHOTO

Looking at the family photo
Dad's pushing a canoe into the lake
Mom's up front apple-bright
I smile back at their fun
Flipping to the next page
I smile again seeing them contemplating the falls

CHILD LEAVING

Wiping flour from her hands
Watching her grandchild step off the curb
Nana waves to the bus driver pulling away
She turns toward the kitchen
Wiping her eyes this time

CELEBRATION

Freckles above a beaming smile
And eyes aglow
She is happy to see me
As though I were her gramps rolling a bike
Honking the horn at her birthday party
She wraps her arms around me

OUT OF THE SHOWER

Hot air blows through me
Steaming the mirror
I reach to trace my initials in the fog
Postponing brushing my teeth

RUDE

She was in a hurry
The white-haired lady with the walker
Struggling to fit herself inside the door
Where I was exiting
She banged me against the wall
And asked me if I were okay
My arm stung like the tears in my eyes
Watching her scoot away

WINTER WOE

Not a dusting of snow, more like ice-laden chunks of frost
Fell across the driveway
And hard for the shovel to heave a pile to the curb

It was evening before I cleared the way
My fingers numb with cold, my back stooped from strain
Craving rest and hot toddy

I was at the door before I realized what I was hearing
Clunk, thud, the scrape of a town plow
Mounting snow in the space where my drive was clean

Still outside, I let the cold shock my senses deeper
Half in disbelief, half in useless anger to what must happen
That I would find myself again shoveling snow to the curb

GHOST

We stood on top of a hill, early in the night
Faced toward the stars, holding hands,
Inhaling the breeze of a soft evening

Had I not been too young
Had he not been too shy
I would have kissed him

Time's wheel has rolled me into later days
Recollections of my past become indistinct
Daily activities forgotten

As I age and blank on faces
As I am uncertain of stairs and how to dress
I am lightheaded, frustrated and alone

I cannot imagine life ahead, what I did today
I do remember, though, an evening on top of a hill
When I was too young and he was too shy

RESPITE

Breathing in the fragrance of honeysuckle
Over a white picket fence
A gardener taking a breather
Leans on his rake
Cursing the sweat rolling from brow to chin
Wishing for a splash in the pool

COOKOUT

The flames of the fired up grill lick chicken legs
The family, smelling the sizzle of barbecue sauce dripping,
Can't wait for the chef to sponge off the table

WORKSHOP

Showing the lathe to me
He spins cherrywood
Grinding grains in his hands
Creating duck decoys
To please the hunter

MISS PRISS

As though Miss Priss were a dragon
She looks at me with her cold glow
I couldn't follow directions squirming in my seat
Couldn't recite the alphabet
Couldn't count to twenty
Miss Priss raises the ruler striking at the desk
Ducking her fire I'm off to the Principal's office

OPEN MIC

Reading at the podium
The book of my poetry shakes in my hand
Halting to say the next line
Tripping over the lyrics
I rush to the end
And leave without applause

ASK

Behind the store counter, she asked
Find what y'all looking fer?
Yes, everything I was looking for
And more
Sounds like y'all not from these parts
You are correct ma'am, I am from Boston
Enjoying beautiful Carolina
The magnolias are sweet in the paahk
And the dandelions are tall in the yaahd

FAN SPIRIT

I will not stop watching the home team
Even though the quarterback deserted
And the head coach denied changes
The line cannot hold long enough
So the wide receivers cannot break free
The line coach calls back the beefy tackle
Who pulled out all the stops at the steak house

UP FROM THE BEACH

Up from the beach
Dead ahead on the sidewalk
The ice cream shack beckons with its neon sign
I picture a hot fudge sundae with nuts and a cherry
And a dollop of whipped cream sliding down my chin
Fingers in my pockets jingle out some quarters
And I plop them gladly in the tip jar

FISHING

I turn my attention away from gulls gliding over white sails
And ask the angler on the pier, what's biting?
Five bass in the pail, one tugging at the line
But look up there
A gull is eyeing my catch of the day

BROWN DOG

Before the sun beams into the morning
Before earthy creatures peep into the day
A coyote lopes through the yard
Looming and foraging where Brown Dog rests
I awaken from dreams
Startled by raucous barking
And spring off the bed
To pat his stiffened fur

GUEST

Delightful to be here
The sand is at my feet
Where sandpipers play
And I can relax
There is a peace settling my thoughts
Hearing the monotony of the ocean rise and fall
On a calm day

KEEPING COOL

Smelling of clean-cut grass and dry earth
He leaned against the porch out of the sun
Right hand still on the mower
Left hand touching my shoulder
It's a scorcher, he whined
And took me inside past the hallway to climb the stairs
We were truants in the heat of afternoon, plopped on a bed
Skipping out from any obligation in quiet relief
Letting the AC breeze over us
Keeping cool

WALK WITH ME

A glimpse of the sun finally is washing away some of the gray. For days the pallor of the sky has matched the dull expanse of ocean underneath. I know the sea from above only by sound when waves roar through the breakwater. It is the kind of gray around me that is damp and sticky. It makes every drawer difficult to open and each door and window hard to shut. It is the gray that sets a mood change and brings energetic thoughts to lie in idle places. Careless reading in cozy corners, passive entertainment in front of a TV, aimless conversation occupy time. This part of neutral summer can leave an indelible mark of laziness.

The assault of August rain is cruel to the shore. Even gentle showers carry pollution and sewerage overload along the beach. This afternoon I am walking a short distance toward the creek. The often-meandering channel heaves swells of detergent and spills bacteria downstream. Before mightier waves could pull this out again, I watch the water bump its way around my toes and cover my ankles in curls of stinking foam. I will hope the tide joins forces with a full moon tonight. Perhaps then, fresher ocean will wash over.

As I make my way across the beach, the urge to look down into the dank, brackish creek is compelling. My feet settle on firm sand which is deeply rippled in some spots by receding waves. I feel as though I am walking on top of a mattress without box springs to push me forward. Since I am already in the water up to my knees, I let my hands drop to the current and slowly move with it. My fingers take in a kind of oil fluence and suddenly, I can't wait to jog back to the cottage for a steaming shower.

Hardly noticeable on my jog are the true and native denizens. There are no screeching gulls, no peeping sandpipers. I see not one jumping fish. The scraping legs of crickets, the annoying hum of insects – they are all quiet. I look to the marsh for signs of egrets and blue herons. Usually, they add their magnificence to the scraggly outline of cattails, reeds, and broad rows of purple and pink growth. But my careful scanning proves frustrating. The meadow seems asleep under a gray quilt.

I do not expect to see children dashing into a refreshing surf with squeals of delight, and I cannot listen to the irritating rhythm of motor boats in search of moorings. The beach is at rest. Shut down. Defined and declared as hazardous to one's health. It has been here all these trillions of days giving us a sense of pride in its beauty, overwhelmed by its gifts. I am looking at the landscape more closely now, seeing who is using and abusing this environment – certainly not hurricanes and rainfall alone.

Stepping quickly over discarded cigarette butts, abandoned potato chip bags, and rotting citrus peels, I marvel at the survival of soft rosehips struggling through sand to root. I cheer for the sparse beach grass which reaches for a cleaner breeze.

Until the evening foghorn calls warning by the rocks of this gray harbor, I will be getting ready for a rainbow. I believe the sun will awaken me tomorrow and I look forward to its return.

PASSAGE

On a sandy expanse where a sea turtle plods
Her hatchlings are led to the sea
What transpires next is nature's ritual
In summer season practiced on the shore
About a mother's letting go, as a mother must
Knowing the fate of her progeny is precarious
Along their journey at the mercy of the ocean

SOLITARY GULL

The gull came back today
His shadow broke the sand
I watched it cross an old sea wall
Then flash beyond the bay
In streaks of white and black he searched
For sisters on the shore
But only plovers are allowed to nest
How happy their choir of fragile voice
Whispers over sand
How sad the screech of the gull
Intrudes through empty sky
Keeping me listening
Hoping he finds a place to rest

SUMMER IS ALMOST OVER

The first disappointment of summer usually follows The Fourth of July when pundits of the new season declare callously that "summer is almost over." What a foreboding thought, as though summer were only a precursor of fall. It is only the last week in June that school finally closes its doors to indoor learning, that libraries, landfill areas, and shopkeepers announce shorter and less convenient hours. It is the last week, too, that I load the station wagon with five excited and anticipating children for the trip to our beach house. For us, Independence Day sets off sparks from winter dreams that will not burn out until Thanksgiving.

COLORS OF AUTUMN

I like the yellow leaves the best swirling on the windshield as I drive to work. A kaleidoscope of crimson and orange already piling on the berm – acorns pitting the hood. There is abundant beauty in the colors of autumn, especially in the back roads where I live. Yet the glory of a pumpkin field and the spook of Halloween pale in the nostalgia of my remembering, shuffling through oak leaves after the rain, slick and vibrant maples kicked aside by my rubber boots as I sauntered home from school. The experience was splendid.

And I was late to set the table.

BOUNTIFUL

Pumpkins are flashing orange brilliance in the warm autumn sun signaling to those passing by that Halloween is coming! They are bumped against each other on crowded vines which twine through acres of farmland. A ton of fiery gourds are harvested and settled beneath the apple stand to taunt customers at 25 cents per pound. Some of those already cooled by a nip from Jack Frost will soon become Jack-o-Lanterns. Others will melt with butter and cinnamon over pie crust.

Though pumpkins are bountiful this season, I could make a pitch for this being the Year of the Pine. The quickest breeze can shake a blizzard of needles off the lofty trees. It is Pine Paradise. Four-legged wildlife preparing for winter need not be greedy in the fetching of fir fruit. Nature has provided abundant avalanches of pine nuts, and I have gathered basketfuls of cones for craft opportunities. My driveway, needless to say, is anything but "needle-less", and when rain came by yesterday it dropped a coniferous cover on this slippery runway. By Thanksgiving my car will have to steer my family toward Grandmother's house through the brown and drifting pine needles.

FOR HEAVEN'S SAKE

When the sky becomes crowded with stars
I bet it's noisy up there
Planets spinning and meteors tumbling
A trillion sparks blare

If a spray of light should fall on me
I'd lie still and make a wish
That there will be peace on Earth
When the stars finally shissh!

SNOW SHADOW

As the moon is rising
Under the glow
Footsteps...quiet
Linger on snow

Beside the thicket
At the end of our way
A dark figure lurks
But does not stay

My eyes would deceive me
Staring through trees
Was a monster coming?
I could not see

I followed its shadow
As the wind started blowing
Down from the north side
Oh, where is it going?

Nearer and nearer
The front porch it loomed
Slogging and panting
I fear I am doomed

Now up to my window
Its frozen nose came
Warming and dripping
And fogging the pane

Yet the smile seemed known
When it curled up its mouth
"Honey, it's Daddy,
 Let me in, I'm home!"

REACHING THE CHANNEL

Day seems night along my way
Undefined paths leading past gray
Toward Moses Creek a sound cuts clear
The tide is stirring the marsh out there
Quickly now across damp sand
My feet can touch a rippled land
Light steps fall, test and sink,
I've reached the spot where egrets drink
Up and down my toes will slide
Warning crabs to scurry and hide
Scrawny life begins to creep
Through salt mud, dank and deep
Mist is rising to leave the water
My journey home will seem much shorter
I plod beside the meadow's shore
Where familiar voices cry from my door
"Mother! Where on earth have you been?"
The channel is turning to open again!
And look way above, a streak of light
Does this tell of a red sky tonight?"

TERMINAL

For a small town
The Greyhound bus is full
The baggage door shuts with a clunk
A cloud of diesel bites the air
And I'm off, braced against a window seat
Passengers stuffed about me in the aisles
Zipping through highway, bumping through towns
The driver calls out the stops
Seeing travelers scatter like angry wasps
I wonder at their rush to get off,
Curious to guess the purpose of their destination
A light snow is distracting me from the pleasure of looking out
And the lull of the road has me sleepy
I hope my travel is not delayed
Because I'm riding to the end of the line

REAL MAN IN A PINK HOUSE?

A shock of sunlight arched across the rooftop of a perspective new home as my husband and I approached its driveway from the back seat of our realtor's BMW. This was the last stop after a weary day's trek through many disappointing "showings." The house had possibilities, I thought, until my husband squinted past the band of golden sky and asked, "Is this house pink?"

Color scheme is important to this man of the Caribbean, a place where yellow and rose hibiscus are pastel appetizers on a plate of real earth colors, like those of mango and citrus which poke through trails of flora in a kaleidoscope of green and tangerine on their way to the sea. Could a man from "The Land of Mountains" who was accustomed to the stark white dwellings of the island, live in a house the same shade as my lipstick?

Hesitating, the realtor took a color cue from the look on her client's face. Her professional voice lilted toward a thoughtful reply, "This house is listed as bisque." Bisque sounded better than pink (known throughout the world as the most feminine of all colors), and the answer propelled us through the front door into a home which we enjoy today as our own. We are still not certain of the true color. Neighbors say it's ecru; friends describe it as apricot, yet it is pink to others. Especially on a bright day, though, when the sun spreads a buttery wash over the clapboards, the house is warm and inviting. And for our money... it is bisque.

BAZAAR INVITATION

November is bazaar month. I didn't exactly make this up. Let's face it. Most holiday shopping starts at an annual bazaar sometime during the shortened days of autumn. Bazaar shopping is not a yard sale, neither flea market nor craft fair. It is an invitation tacked on bulletin boards, sent by flyer, or posted on telephone poles promoting a seasonal shopping experience. If you think that bargaining for mismatched, possibly defective items donated to the "White Elephant Nook" or vying with a neighbor for the last tray of Congo Bars at the "Baked Goods Table" is a stressful yet rewarding activity, imagine the preparation involved in setting up such an event. Know that busy hands and creative minds equal success.

Church bazaars are one thing, though the Boy Scouts, Parent Teachers Association, Senior Centers, etc., have managed their own version of cottage industry, hoping to bring money into their organization. The local vocational school is a favorite of mine. Every year they run a theme for their "Homemade Items Booth." Last year it was Gingerbread Houses, edible, sweet dwellings put together with TLC and a tweak of imperfection which means they are the genuine handmade article ... no assembly in Sri Lanka, no imports from China. This year, it's Bird Houses, snug little abodes painted green with glued-on pine cones and a tiny silver bell which jingles above the entrance. I suppose the sparrows will want to know when they have a visitor. Instead of answering the bazaar invitation, I might just put a few bucks into the Salvation Army kettle or make a drop off at Toys for Tots. But then, the local vocational students may not have their ski trip this winter, and I won't have a new bird house.

YARD SALE-ING

My sister-in-law insisted on rescuing me from my Saturday morning task of pulling weeds from an overburdened garden. She would introduce me to the fine art of yard sale-ing instead. "You're never going to find the perfect vase (pronounced vaahz) for your foyer if you don't get out and look for it."

Jeanette's mouth curled into an assuming, militant smile. Simultaneously, her left hand shoved the garden spade into the garage as her right arm marched me to the passenger seat of her 4-wheel jeep. At the turn of a key, we headed out on our mission, bumping over potholes, veering continuously from crooked mailboxes plunked on the sides of country roads, until we dead-ended somewhere past South County.

Even at mid-morning, flickering neon lights waved a multitude of yard-salers into one and a half acres of open market at Hollow Grove. As I trudged through damp grass in open-toed sandals, a quick glance at mile long tables wedged under lofty pines, which, by the way, kept spitting cones at us in sudden wind gusts, suggested a long day of exploration.

The smell of old furniture hung in the air as Jeanette maneuvered me from bargain to bargain. I felt a shiver of familiarity when we snaked our way around small appliance displays, noting that it was quite some time ago that I discarded the same blender and corn popping machines. Yet among a stalagmite of arts and crafts, tacky exhibits of household items, books, and vintage clothing, Jeanette found just the right knick-knack for her mantel, the prettiest welcome wreath for her door, and dozens of must have articles for immediate gratification.

Hours later, as I swung tired legs into the jeep, I revealed my find to Jeanette. When she asked, "What in hell is THAT?" I proudly replied, "It's a tab lifter, a small plastic gadget for opening soda cans." "But you don't drink soda," she laughed.

Like a good soldier, though, I have a plan. I am never going to use this engineering marvel. It will be kept in a cool, dry place, undisturbed in its original packaging. Sometime into the future, if the Antiques Road Show visits Boston, I will bring my discovery to the plastic's device expert. In front of a gasping audience, I hope to realize that this 25-cent item, manufactured circa 2022, is now worth 25,000 dollars. Then I will hire a gardener to weed my plants. If I have not already done so, I can use the free time to go yard sale-ing in search of the perfect vaahz.

DON'T CALL ME LATE ANYMORE

Thunderheads stacked up over city buildings send bullets of rain pinging onto the windshields of cars as they screech to a stop on opposite sides of Washington Street. A quick check in the rearview mirror reassures me that the metallic green SUV which has been tailgating my vehicle through Providence made the red light without compromise to anyone's fender. Despite the weather and traffic, I am feeling lucky today, and if directions to this morning's Punctuality Training Session are accurate, I might be on time ... for once.

You see, there is this demon in me, a taunting and distracting force called Procrastination. It lurks in my subconscious ready to delay and deter me at the mere suggestion of a deadline. I admit it. For most of my life, Procrastination has caused me to be apologetic, even sorry, for my habitual tardiness. But nobody ever really scolded me about not being on time, probably because I had such great "stand-by" excuses: I didn't feel well and woke up late worked okay when I was in school. Not to brag, but I was late for class nearly every day of my senior year, and I lived just across the street from the school. Later, inclement weather and traffic jams became the preferred reasons for showing up late. Then it was the dog or the kids ... or my mother called from Idaho just as I was leaving.

Rain falls in soft drizzles as I arrive for my training. I am a little tardy. And all because Procrastination lured me into the drive-thru lane at Dunkin' Donuts where I had to wait ages for the Grind-of-the-Day. I expect the trainer to read me the riot act. Instead, he gently allows me into the session, asking me about my lifestyle, sizing me up. He is confident that I can get rid of this devil of a problem. "It is not in your genes, afterall, he says. Procrastination is just putting off the inevitable." Slowly at first, he begins a kind of exorcism. He rambles on in a lecture about punctuality, making me repeat key words like prompt and timely. Words move quickly into a volley of scolding phrases. He's hurling them at me now, so fast all I can catch is "leave earlier" "stay focused" "have goals."

I am taking his advice immediately. My goal is to leave early so I can be home in time for dinner. With intentional lack of interest about everything except the road ahead, I stay focused until reaching the intersection at Washington Street. As amber turns to red on the overhead traffic light, I notice a flashing yellow arrow pointing left ... **DETOUR**, it warns. Wouldn't you know it!

BED AND BREAKFAST

Forget the Sheraton Suites Hotel with its indelibly luxurious surroundings, its exciting cuisine offerings and critically acclaimed service. The hottest place on the South Shore to experience rest and relaxation these days is in the casual atmosphere of Ye Ole Bed & Breakfast Inn. Or so my neighbor said when she handed me the brochure. I was ready for all it promised – the ultimate indulgence in country living, everything homemade, quaint, comfortable accommodations among a tapestry of luscious gardens and rolling meadows.

Hot, diffuse light from the July sun already sizzled into early morning when I decided to take the highway which should bring my neighbor and me to a cool sunset on the front porch of that honest-to-goodness, turn-of-the-century inn. I felt like a kid again, cruising in the driver's seat of my first car, liberated, singing with the voice on the radio above the drone of passing 18-wheelers.

I think it was a sparrow. I am not an ornithology expert. But a bird got caught in the grill of my vehicle as I was slicing across four lanes of traffic to make the great "merge" before the highway splits through the city. Anyway, our trip was a little delayed while we scraped the headlights and windshield of feathers. Until some hours later, when we broke free of the highway and found ourselves winding through miles of isolated road, did the idea of plopping on a featherbed under a handsome quilt take on heightened appeal. Finally, just as the sun met Earth in a smooth line announcing dusk, I pulled up to Ye Ole B & B.

The owner sat on a splintered bench chewing something brown. His only companion, a slick-looking canine, shot past us, lifted her hind leg beside a spittoon, then growled in huge relief. "Pay no mind to Hunker, she's just a puppy." Still, a Rottweiler is a Rottweiler, I thought. My neighbor signed the register and we were hustled to Room #14. We met the guests in Room #15. They were chasing twin toddlers in the hallway which connected our rooms. I bumped into the teenage brother quite by accident, just moments after I discovered we would be sharing the same bathroom.

It took but a minute to survey our quarters. Right away I chose top bunk. Where spiders had cleverly woven webs into a thin braided rug, rested the only other furniture. So, to be fair, I let my friend have the two-drawer bureau. On top lay the decorator's touch – a plastic vase shedding an arrangement of dried flowers ... probably salvaged from the rolling meadows.

I think it was when the teen yelled, "Hey, Dad! Dad, don't this place have cable?" that my friend dropped her head and cried. I told her, "Okay, cheer up, tomorrow will be different." And it was. After a six-a.m. breakfast of biscuits and gooseberry jelly, we headed north from a rural lane singing, loud, above the murmurs of crickets and mourning doves.

        1-800-SHERATON   tra la la la la!

SIX MONTHS LATER

A force unknown to me caused my feet to bring the rest of my body into the small room. As I stepped out of the sunshine, though, I determined not to let my nerves get the best of me. I kept thinking, just want this to be over.

When my eyes got used to the darkness of deep green walls and dull commercial carpeting, I saw them. Two of them, girls in their early twenties with starched faces and crisp voices, looking like they just graduated from the College of Arts and Attitudes. The one with reddish hair acknowledged my entrance with a snap of her ponytail while the other raised a pointed finger and indicated, "I'll be with you in a moment."

Behind a sliding window, however, the girls continued to answer wailing telephones. A half hour of moments went by before I turned my attention from reading outdated issues of Newsweek to counting rows of tweed squares on gray chairs lined against the far wall. In the next half hour of moments, I had time to play with my pocket calculator and write out a grocery list. Then, just as I contemplated a visit to the unisex restroom, a clipboard was placed under my chin. Looking up I heard, "Fill in all the information and return this form to me." I caught the pen which danced from the clipboard on a yard of tangled string and began to fill in the blanks.

At the same time, breaking from his mother's hold, a young boy slammed the outer door and leaped into the unoccupied chair beside me. Nothing new about kids fidgeting and jiggling around when they have to wait. And so it was with him. He rocked and bounced, and tapped his shoes together making sure to hit my chair with each beat. This youngster was both talented and ambidextrous. He could whistle Old Macdonald Had a Farm and snap his fingers on both hands simultaneously. He knew how to make repugnant noises while sweeping his arms from side to side. His grandest sweep knocked my purse into the air spinning it to the floor like a toy top. I dove after it, loose change whizzing past me like shrapnel, lipsticks rolling under seats, parachutes of store receipts landing everywhere.

There was a sudden silence in which I crawled toward my scattered belongings, broken only by someone who raised a pointed finger above me and curtly announced, "The dentist will see you ... in a moment."

UPON OUR VISITOR'S STOPPING

He made the trip this October by rail and on foot, wandering through small woods, by lily ponds and cranberries running wild, and ended up under the comforting thickness of the big cedar outside the south window. Father stoked a lazy fire and gesturing with the sizzling poker, directed Annie and me to hide the good scotch. There was a pounding on the door, and at last the window was raised. Father asked, 'What do you want?' 'I want to stay here all night.' 'All right – stay there.' And down went the window. Father's humor, dry as cured herring and stolen from the wit of Daniel Webster was repeated every autumn upon our visitor's stopping.

The night grew raw but clear. We could see Dumpling Rock Light flash one-four-three-one-four-three (I Love You, I Love You) as evening whispered shadows over the dunes and quieted the harbor. Our guest, having dodged the low-studded beams of the den, tucked himself against fat pillows on an overstuffed chair. Then raising his arms as a deacon might before a sermon, he began to romance us with familiar tales. The mantel clock ticked on as we were taken past forgotten burying grounds and told of folks lying there, of hunting and fishing in ancient places, and old houses that welcomed captains home from the sea. He rambled about weather and hurricanes and his own relatives, particularly his uncle who lived to be a hundred and ten. "The poor old man was so shrunk and withered, he used to sleep in a baby's crib."

First Annie yawned then myself. We said good-night respectfully, but instead of heading to our bedroom, Annie and I disappeared into the pantry where we settled ourselves on top of bulky lobster pots. Through the open door we saw Father put up the fire screen and watched the two men turning around and around thoroughly toasting themselves with the warmth. Glasses clinked as old friends honored each other in what seemed an endless salute, when suddenly the guest stepped down from the hearth and blurted:

> WE'RE FOOT-slog-slog-slog-slogging' over Africa
> FOOT-foot-foot-foot-sloggin' over Africa
> (Boots-boots-boots-boots-movin' up and down again)
> There's no discharge in the war!

The compelling sound of Kipling's rhyme exploded as two voices coming out of the den bounced from all about. They were marching with spare andirons carried on their shoulders like weapons, clompfing as though in soldier's shoes across the hardwood floor....

> Don't-don't don't-don't-look at what's in front of you.
> (Boots-boots-boots-boots-movin' up and down again!),
> Men-men-men-men-men go mad from watchin' em n'
> there's no discharge in the war!

Verse after verse, they shouted and clamored until conscious of the fire dying, final words were recited.

A slight rustling in the cedars awakened us to an early morning fog. Annie and I found the two pennies our visitor had left us, distorted and dirty coins flattened by a locomotive.

We toppled them into the old jar where we used to keep sea glass thinking about all the pennies we had collected over the years. Quietly, softly, as the muted whistle of a train faded somewhere into the distance, Annie and I brewed Father's coffee.

ATTIC MAN

I have a little house snuggled among the hills of Indigo Valley. It stays cold most of the year where I am, usually April wind shakes through the woods before I can tell the birch from the snow. There is a mean spirit in the air that whips onto the land in late afternoon and settles in shadows of deep purple. It suits my mood perfectly. I have craved the valley since I was a young girl spending holidays here with my grandfather. I remember he was a burly man, a Davy Crockett type, strong yet winsome, with flame-colored hair he let droop around a face of rugged good looks. It was easy to accept my inheritance when he passed away. Of course, I am not a true native, but the sense of mountain life in its simplicity touches my heart; the feel of its mystery impresses my soul. I am perpetually in awe of my surroundings and amused by the people who live among such splendor-like my friend, Damien Bates. Haven't I rubbed it into old Mr. Bates that I enjoy early evenings whenever he gripes that winter cheats him of a full day? Rhetorically, my imagination sparks like lightening in the quiet of long nights when memories take me to lost places and dreams seem real. On the occasion of his stopping by, I am glad for Mr. Bates' company. He is a gifted man, his voice lilting and magical, fit for telling tales.

Just as I am thinking there is nothing quite like a bottle of Chardonnay, great books, and a pleasant fire in the hearth on a blustery eve, Matches leaped from the sofa onto the marble table scudding to a halt where the last half dozen of my Martha Stewart candles flickered in his wake.

"Get down, naughty cat. What do you want, to set the house on fire?"

Surprised by my reprimand, Matches hissed through stiff black whiskers like a rattler, arched his back to the ceiling and stared at the window. Whatever turned those sober dark eyes tiger-bright deserved a closer look. When I switched on the lamp by the porch, evening peered at me through a shimmer of light. I inched the door open against a gray landscape; the peaks of the hills were vague, just a faint outline on the horizon. The air was different, heavy and damp, and without a breath of wind forced the pines and oak into bleak silence. Before I could think to slap up the latch, Matches shot past me bumping the door shut. I caught a glimpse of his tail as he hunched inside one of the flower urns. I was mad, mad enough to curse out loud, "Damn cat, come back here!" I wanted to add, "or else" but then, Matches is my precious pet. He did not budge. Matches can stay out all night if he wants to, but I plan to brave the weather from the inside. Ramming my shoulder against the door and pushing with my foot did not open the door, neither did twisting the knob every which way. I tried again, shoving, and kicking. I considered the proverbial throw a stone in the window trick, but sliding my hand through spikes of glass was as unappealing as having to repair the broken pane.

By now I was washed with mist and my hair snarled in a wet mess. Overhead, the light pulsed and dimmed. Probably I hadn't replaced the bulb in ages. A sigh, and two shivers later, I decided to look for a stone.

Perhaps it was a lucky stone I found and kneaded through my fingers. A voice called to me from the walkway, and then, the familiar clomp of Damien Bates' footsteps.

He wore red, fire-engine red, a hunter's jacket and cap that defied the fog rolling around his silhouette. The grin on his face stretched his beard ear to ear and creased his forehead in deep wrinkles. "Forget to pay your electric bill?" "Or, maybe I forgot to change a light bulb."

His hand was amazingly warm and stayed clasped over mine in tender greeting before he gripped the door knob. It turned smoothly as Mr. Bates gestured with an open arm inviting me into my own house. "Please join me for a glass of wine and some chit-chat." I gave him a jittery smile and tossed the stone before hurrying over the threshold.

The foyer spread into the den where Mr. Bates plunked himself next to the hearth in an overstuffed chair, the sort that shouts, Grandfather bought me! But the butter cream walls recently painted complement the honey-oak floor adding lightness to a clunky display of antique furniture. The stairway leading up to a large attic space is an ornate curve of mahogany where gargoyles are sculpted into the newel post. They cling to the wood with clawed hands and stare down with eyes carved to see in every direction. What have they seen, I wonder, in the years when Grandfather lived here. The attic was once my make-believe place. I climbed the stairs to play and sort through whatever was up there to pique my fantasy. Grandfather's belongings lay in open boxes: pelted garments and fur lined hats, snowshoes, and hiking gear. I noticed Mr. Bates scan the steps before he remarked, "Lousy night and it was a dang-lousy-short day, don't you think, Cassandra?"

"A day is twenty-four hours, no matter how you pass the time, no matter what the season." "Well, well, Cassie, you are spilling out attitude all over your words, being logical when I'm crabbing. Why the sour disposition, is something wrong?"

My breathy reply explained how Matches bolted outside and refuses to return at my calling. "I don't see the point of worrying about that feline. The chances of him not scratching at the door sometime tonight are as weak as a baby's bones. For once, let's try to spend an evening without him scampering and meowing.

I held crystal wine glasses while Mr. Bates offered to uncork the Chardonnay. For an instant his eyes met mine. I felt a power from that gaze, a prickle of heat from electric blue eyes. It made me think he could see right into my mind. The cork released with a pop as quickly as the moment passed. Still being flushed, though, I sat on the braided rug away from the fire. Mr. Bates stepped over and clinked his glass against mine as is the custom. "Let us lift up our glasses against evil forces." I toasted back to him asking, "Do you have an aversion to all cats in general, or is it just Matches you dislike?" "Why, Cass, I believe your animal, like other cats, is just cunning." His tone scaled down an octave as he emphasized, absolutely cunning.

There was an ominous rumble overhead when Mr. Bates rocked back into his chair. Rain began to spit across the window, easy at first, then steadily beating like a metronome. After a sudden crack of lightening, Damien Bates raised his eyebrows thoughtfully. I would like to tell you a story. It seems a night for spinning a yarn."

I bent forward to pick another canape and sip some wine, then eased down again to listen.

"In another time, the mountains were taller and the forest denser. Men hunted in the hills and women worked in their homes. There was harmony in this arrangement passed on from generation to generation. And through the years tales were told in the village conceived from a plain folk who knew the power of nature."

I taste the water, clear and cold, but not enough to keep aflutter of snowflakes from melting in the ripples of this quiet stream. I let it pour over my soiled hands while the other men pull in the bounty from the week's trappings. I smell pine, spruce, and some musky trees blending with the scent of freshly killed rabbit. A deer lay on the path, his carcass prepared for the trek home, legs bound, his head crooked slightly. The women and children will be satisfied with our catch.

Voices chant in the distance, songs from companions, deep and bold and male. I want to join in, but sounds echo back and forth and I cannot reach their source. My feet slog across damp earth and bring me to a place where fallen leaves and logs poke through a carpet of white. I decide to rest under the shelter of their branches. Suddenly, now, the sky thickens. A wind swells into a funnel of violet. Dark, dark it rises. As I look up, the forest splits open in a burst of snow that shocks my eyes.

I see mothers and sisters. They are waiting for us to come home, going about their daily tasks. I see my mother smoothing wrinkles from a handsome quilt, and I see her sister setting our table with bright linen. It is their daughters I hear, screeching and romping with kittens that won't be still in their laps. So lovely is their pleasure that gathers all in laughter. Yet there is a force here, terrible, and impending.

Then ... see them. Innocent at first, sleek, lean mountain cats that surround the children and linger in the play yard. Abruptly, the frolic stops. Children's names are called and not answered. I am paralyzed in the silence as if I know even before I see the jagged teeth, the quick bites, the wounds, before black shadows slink back into the hills.

There in the valley, the children sleep. Beside them are the hunters and their wives. Lanterns sway in their hands, and, as if in the clutch of destiny are hurled into the night. Flames and smoke billow to the rooftops. I feel the roaring heat. And seeing my village burn, I weep.

I drank in the sound of his voice, sometimes low and ragged, somehow exotic and mesmerizing like embers in the fireplace touching every corner of the room with light and shade.

"Fascinating story, Mr. Bates, but that can't be the end of the tale. What happened to the hunter?" The question caused Mr. Bates to tremble as he checked his watch. "Ah, I've got to go." There was no need for me to protest. Rain clamored onto the roof and banged into the shutters convincing Mr. Bates to delay his departure. He exchanged a frown for a shrug that raised his shoulders almost to his chin. "Well, all right, make coffee, Cassandra."

The pot sputtered to full perk as Mr. Bates measured a second teaspoon of sugar into a Dresden China cup. Neither of us spoke for awhile. The intense look of Mr. Bates suggested he welcomed a chance to weave together the final threads of his story before he said another word. In the obvious quiet a wave of excitement gushed over me. I was poised on the edge of my seat anticipating wildly to hear the unravelling of some secret. Finally, he set his cup on the table, then took mine from me and did the same with it.

Mr. Bates cleared his throat uncomfortably. When he managed to speak, emotion broke from his voice charming me back to the story.

Snow falls in swirling gusts and smothers my footprints as I trudge across the mountain like a man in a trance. Am I walking in circles? "Down! Keep going down." It's a frantic scream in my mind orienting me through an impossible maze of frozen trees. I persuade myself not to run but move steadily on. I realize nothing more than the cold of the forest floor until I come to an open way. The sky thins where a gloomy light from the moon hangs above me. I focus on it edging my steps to the bottom.

Warmth, the golden glimmer of dawn flows over me. A figure moves near me, slowly. Shape without form begins to solidify, slowly. I can make out every detail – the long coat of weathered suede bordered with fur, the trapper's belt, fastened high under his breasts. Not so clear is the face, veiled by a flop of crimson hair. The hand I reached for tightens on mine and am pulled along a pattern of tracks which mark the path to a small, cozy home in the valley.

The rain slowed to a drizzle in the same calm manner Mr. Bates was concluding his story. His words dragged into murmurs, at times almost inaudible slurs until he fell silent.

In quiet misery I live in the attic above my rescuer. A changed man now in a space like some bottomless gorge of endless nights, I retreat ... and remember.

Flames like tongues of copper and gold licked around the logs springing points of brilliance everywhere. As Mr. Bates turned near the window, his profile leaped and quivered in the illumination. He looked like one of the gargoyles on the stairs, his eyes leering in mock-ing distortion. Was he contemplating the weather? I couldn't tell.

I heard a whimper and what sounded like scratching. It was a welcome relief to stand in the doorway and have my precious pet scamper toward me. When Damien Bates rolled his eyes on us, Matches hunkered down purring loudly and locked his tail around my leg. He looked as innocent as anything.

I accompanied Mr. Bates to the walkway and watched him disappear into the trees. The overhead fixture had burned out, but the night was not dark. Streaks of lavender graciously paled the sky to let the moon out. Though my friend and I did not talk about his story tonight, I have a feeling his tale will tumble through my head in thoughts and dreams until morning. And morning is a long time from now.

www.ingramcontent.com/pod-product-compliance
Lightning Source LLC
Chambersburg PA
CBHW021131080526
44587CB00012B/1241